# THE DEFINITIVE
## (and Totally True)
# HISTORY
### of DOOR
# SLAMMING

by I.B. Schlammen

RP Minis®
Hachette Book Group
1290 Avenue of the Americas, New York, NY 10104
www.runningpress.com
@Running_Press

First Edition: May 2022

Published by RP Minis, an imprint of Perseus Books, LLC, a subsidiary of Hachette Book Group, Inc. The RP Minis name and logo is a registered trademark of the Hachette Book Group.

The publisher is not responsible for websites (or their content) that are not owned by the publisher.

ISBN: 978-0-7624-7992-4

# The Big Slam Theory

The beat of a butterfly's wings. The lapping of a single wave. An insignificant leaf falling from a mighty oak. Small behaviors ripple across space and time and change the course of history. (Deep stuff, huh?) But one action has impacted human civilization more than any other:

the DOOR SLAM. (At least that's my theory, and I'm stickin' to it.)

Think about it . . . The sudden *WHOOSH* of a door swinging. The haunting *CREAK* of its hinges. The "Big *BANG*," if you will, of the door slamming shut. The sounds are unmistakable.

Primal. One might even say, as this historian does, *instinctual*.

And it's no wonder. Since the dawn of doors, men and women—and Cro-Magnon men and Cro-Magnon women—have sought to slam them. Sure, I know, it's a far-fetched theory, but one cannot simply slam the door shut on the possibility.

And so, fellow Door-Slamming Aficionados, I present to you *The Definitive (and Totally True) History of Door Slamming,* a compact—yet impactful—tome highlighting momentous moments in the history of the door slam and its jarring (and *ajar*-ing) impact on world events. Through painstaking research (believe me, *very* little evidence exists for this stuff), this book traces door slamming's origins from the Prehistoric Period to the Middle Ages to Modern

Civilization. Along the way, you'll discover believe-it-or-not facts about door slamming (I, for one, choose to believe!) and uncover answers to history's greatest door-slamming mysteries.

# The Nean-door-thals

Few Door-Slamming Historians (if others actually exist) would agree on the earliest-known Door Slammers. It was, after all, the Prehistoric Period, an era prior to any kind historical record. Seriously, like, nobody really knows *anything* for sure (which is lucky for me, to be honest). However, one thing's for almost-certain . . . At some point, an early human-oid was crawling along and decided, "Hey, maybe I should just stand up and walk on these two legs. I could move a lot faster, and my knees wouldn't hurt as much."

So they did.

Bipedalism gave early humans—whom I've termed *Nean-door-thals* (because it's my book, after all)—many distinct advantages over other species. The most significant? Their ability to slam doors grew *EXPONENTIALLY*.

Walking on two legs freed up Nean-door-thal's hands, a trait necessary for proper door slamming. If evidence did exist (which it doesn't), I'd assume that this evidence would suggest cave doors (had they also existed) would've been remarkably heavy. Repeatedly slamming these giant, stone doors could've helped early humans build muscles in their biceps and forearms and, perhaps, dexterity in their fingers and thumbs—ultimately leading to the ability to use tools and weapons.

(Like I said, it's pre-history, after all. Anything could've happened . . .)

Another evolutionary advantage of door slamming? Survival itself, if you can believe that. (And why wouldn't you?) From woolly mammoths to saber-toothed tigers, dangerous and deadly beasts populated Nean-door-thal's world. With little protection—except for a few measly sticks and rock shards—early humans were much more *flight* than *fight*, assuredly. And where did these unibrowed cowards flee? Although absolutely no evidence exists, somé believe (i.e. *this* guy) behind a heavy cave door—a slammed-shut one, most likely.

Following that logic (Again, why wouldn't you?), door slamming was the ultimate evolutionary advantage. And, over time, fewer and fewer Non-Door Slammers survived, leading to their eventual extinction.

(Still skeptical? Take a DNA spit test, why don't you. Nothing about Non-Door Slammers in there, that's for sure.)

# The Door to Civilization

Ironically, Door Slammers actually *opened* the door to modern civilization. From the Ancient Greeks to the Roman Empire, door slamming became an important aspect of newly formed societies. Again, although no evidence exists, one could speculate that door slamming was crucial for trapping gladiators inside the Roman Colosseum. (I mean, they obviously wouldn't have just stayed there like free-range chickens . . . . ) As for Ancient Greeks, they utilized door slamming to shut out commoners from their aristocratic bathhouses. (Bathhouses for all!) Even to this day, power and privacy endure as critical components of door slamming.

As with military combat, door slamming remained a hand-to-hand task throughout much of early history. Few technological advances existed until the

Medieval Period. During this time, door slamming became essential to military defense. Although castle walls protected kings and queens from flaming cannon-balls and thieving Robin Hoods, the high stone walls had one major drawback: large, heavy doors. These doors were nearly impossible for a single Englishman to close, let alone an entire battalion. Forget sneaking inside with Trojan Horses; before castle doors could be slammed shut, a whole enemy army (or even a slow-trotting Little John) could've walked inside with ease.

The solution? A mechanical door-slamming device! Although known today as a "drawbridge," at least one historian (OK, *me*) believes this chain-and-weight invention was originally known as "Ye Ol' Door Slammer," a simple—yet sophisticated—advancement in door-slamming technology and a deterrent to castle invaders everywhere.

# The Dark Ages of Door Slamming

This door-slamming renaissance, if you will, was short-lived. Soon after, door slamming and Door Slammers alike declined throughout Europe and the world. Today, this period is known as the Dark Ages. (*Dun Dun Duhnnn . . .*)

The term alone is a strong indication of its relation to the action of door slamming. Although door slamming had advantages prior to the invention of electricity, including safety and security, it also had an unavoidable disadvantage: darkness. A slammed door didn't allow for natural light, after all. And, with little light for reading and writing (Ever tried reading by candlelight?), people avoided intellectual and literary pursuits. Instead, they often decided to, well, just take naps, which eventually led to economic declines throughout Western Civilization.

Slammed doors also introduced another hazard to early people: lack of ventilation. Although slamming a door on that neighbor offering a bushel of turnips certainly felt good, as it would today, closed-door conditions led to many illnesses—even, perhaps, contributing to the infamous Black Plague. (Although, admittedly, my sourcing here is rather thin.)

No wonder door slamming fell out of fashion for hundreds of years afterward—many of history's greatest Door Slammers tragically succumbed to illness.

# Modern Door Slamming

For most of history, one type of door slamming dominated: the ENTRANCE SLAM. This type of door slamming occurs when a person slams a door upon hastily entering a residence or room, such as retreating from saber-tooths and/or turnip-pushers. In the modern age, another type of door slamming came to dominate door-slamming culture: the EXIT SLAM.

Like an entrance, the exit slam has certain advantages. Most often this type of door slam is utilized to show frustration with another, including people or animals.

In fact, one of the earliest recorded cases of exit door-slamming occurred in Chicago, Illinois, on October 8, 1871. On that night, a woman, who for our purposes we'll call Mrs. O'Leary (because that's her name), struggled to milk her old cow. After growing increasingly frustrated, Mrs. O'Leary stormed out of the barn, slamming the heavy door behind her, causing the entire barn to shake and the lantern to fall onto a nearby pile of hay.

The result: the Great Chicago Fire (which was really anything but great)!

In fact, many unintentionally consequences of door slamming have changed the course of human history. Did a thoroughly slammed door trigger the eruption of Mount Vesuvius? Almost certainly. Did Neil Armstrong and Buzz

Aldrin close the door on Michael Collins' moonwalk chances? It's possible. Did door slamming lead to the creation of the internet? Well, probably not. But, then again, never shut the door on the possibility.

# Culture Slam

For years, door slamming in the modern office environment was as critical as the fax machine. Big wigs in corner offices often slammed their doors for a lunch-hour cocktail or after a stress-inducing stock market drop. In fact, some believe the term stock market "crash" is, indeed, a reference to the sound of a slamming door. (Don't quote me on that.)

More recently, however, the integration and acceptance of open-door and open floor plan office policies has threatened to make door slamming extinct. No event has jeopardized door slamming this much since the swinging saloon-door craze of the Wild West or, more recently, the barn door craze of remodeled suburban homes. (Don't even get me started on revolving doors!)

Thankfully, the *Desktop Door Slam*

kit is the latest evolution in the long tradition of door slamming.

Office workers everywhere can now experience the relieving sensation of slamming shut their own door, including those lowly cubical dwellers among us. It also eliminates most major disadvantages of door slamming, both historical and modern, while maintaining advantages like stress relief. (Of course, the minor threat of a saber-tooth attack still remains.)

So, fellow Door-Slamming Aficionados, it appears we are at a critical juncture in the history of door slamming. Will door slamming evolve into new, more modern forms, like the *Desktop Door Slam* kit? Or are we entering another door slam Dark Age, where door slamming eventually falls into extinction. I, for one, hope not.

Think about it . . . Where would we be as a human species without epic events like Roman gladiators being eaten by lions, the Black Plague, or the Great Chicago Fire—? OK, not the best examples, but I'm sure there are some.

And besides, if door slamming didn't exist, what would happen to all of us Door-Slamming Historians? (All one of us, that is.) We'd be out of work.

So keep slamming those doors, Door Slammers! Whether exiting or entering, large doors or small doors, the mighty door slam will ripple across space and time and continue to change the course of human history.

Case closed (with a thoroughly hearty slam).

This book has been bound using
handcraft methods and Smyth-sewn
to ensure durability.

Designed by Celeste Joyce.

Illustrated by Gabriel Hollington.